What I Did

My Year as I Made It

Sue Messruther

Black & White Version

First Printing, 2018
ISBN-13: 978-1722633684
ISBN-10: 1722633689

Why this book?

Over the years, I had really wished that I had kept notes or remembered something that at the time was very special or often a lesson learnt but then forgot all of the little details.

Many times I try to remember things that I had done so that I could tell my children and although I could remember most of the details it was the little things that I had forgotten and they are now lost forever!

As I am a great believer in "our life is what we make it", the title for the first in this series "My Year as I Made It" was easy now I just needed to make sure that I keep writing and then I can give my journals to my children and they will be able to read how I felt, what I achieved, what I tried to achieve and all my hopes and dreams for that year!

Now it is your turn, record your life as and when it happens and what how you grow through the year and achieve things that you never thought you would, then at the end of the year you can take time to reflect and realise your life is what you made it!

The year is

____

This journal belongs to:

____

A little about me:

____
____
____
____
____
____
____
____
____
____

My photo:

Contents

January

February

March

April

May

June

July

August

September

October

November

December

About The Author

Born in Adelaide, South Australia, Sue Messruther has written many well-reviewed books, a good mix for adults and children as Sue is a mother of 6 children and currently 6 grandchildren. She loves her allotment and spends many hours weeding, watering and planning next year's crops, even here her humour shines through as her allotment has street signs!

She has created many adult colouring books, journals and organisers these just continue to grow as inspiration guides her onto the next book.

Sue's children's books are a true delight as she composes all of the images around the stories she creates. Her bestselling children's volume sets include the Just For Kids series, Alien Caper Encounters series and the Dogs, Cats & All Other Animals and let's not forget Messruther's stand-alone titles which include Santa's Christmas: The Year the Sleigh Broke Down, Christmas Home Made Cookie Gifts, and 30 Best Breads from Around the World.

Sue enjoys creating & colouring in her Adult Colouring Books & Journals, some of these have space to add extra doodles, others that are simple and then many images that are challenging! So she does create and use her own books, in fact many of the journals were created because she had a need for them and her colouring books she needed these for the dementia patients she looks after in her full time job.

Messruther has also contributed writings to the books Thorns to be Thankful For and Skill Share both of which became best sellers in the first week of publication.

There are always more books in the creation cycle for example a new children's series currently in various stages is the Play Time Books, which forthcoming from the author, of which Come Find Me Under The Sea is the first to arrive in this series followed by Back In Time With Dinosaurs and then It's A Dog's Life. Titles after this are yet to be determined!

Messruther has lived in Cairns, Queensland, Australia and now currently resides in Scarborough, North Yorkshire, England, with her family and Oscar, an Old English Sheep puppy of gigantic proportions, (Digby is a constant thought and fear, and will Oscar grow that big!) Thankfully, his growth has slowed down now so Digby II is safe from reality!

As with everyone, her life and inspirations grow on a daily basis so the future is looking very creative indeed to follow up with new titles you can contact Sue Messruther on her facebook page https://www.facebook.com/suemessruther.author/ she would love to hear from you and you can follow her progress.

Other Titles

Journals

My Christmas List Journal

Best & Worst Days Pocket Diary

Saying It Pocket Coloring Journal

You know your cat is the center of your life when.

The Collective Useful Diary – Family

Monthly To Do Journal – Dooley Me

Monthly To Do Journal – Whimsical Me

Monthly To Do Journal – My Heart

Monthly To Do Journal – My Blossom

Monthly To Do Journal – Oh My Timber

Monthly To Do Journal – My Trekking

Monthly To Do Journal – Posy Me

Expressing Myself Journal

Awakening my soul family

Awakening my soul yourself

I wish I had said that!

All That I Did - My Year As I Made It

I Did It My Way - My Year As I Made It

As I See It - My Year As I Made It

What I Did - My Year As I Made It

I Did What? - My Year As I Made It

I Achieved - My Year As I Made It

All That I Achieved - My Year As I Made It

I Achieved It My Way - My Year As I Made It

I Did It! - My Year As I Made It

I Said and I Did It - My Year As I Made It

My Progress - My Year As I Made It

My Life - My Year As I Made It

Bit By Bit - My Year As I Made It

Step By Step - My Year As I Made It

One Step at a Time - My Year As I Made It

One Day at a Time - My Year As I Made It

Month by Month - My Year As I Made It

Day by Day - My Year As I Made It

Through The Year - My Year As I Made It

Every Day Is New - My Year As I Made It

I Made It! - My Year As I Made It

Another Year - My Year As I Made It

Organisers

My Organiser - That's Life

My Organiser - I Rule

My Organiser - For The Weekends

My Organiser - Fantasy

My Organiser - Flower power

My Organiser - Puppy love

My Organiser - Perrrrfect Days